Original title:
Sheltered in the Walls

Copyright © 2025 Creative Arts Management OÜ
All rights reserved.

Author: Evelyn Hartman
ISBN HARDBACK: 978-1-80587-102-6
ISBN PAPERBACK: 978-1-80587-572-7

Lost Yet Found Amidst Four Walls

In corners I find all my missing socks,
The cat thinks my shoes are great for mocks.
Dust bunnies dance in a whimsical parade,
While I search for the remote, my fondest charade.

I trip on a rug that is far too proud,
It laughs as I tumble, just like a crowd.
Amongst these mishaps, I chuckle aloud,
For every small blunder, I'm always enshroud.

The Calm Surface Beneath

Beneath the calm lies a rubber duck,
It squeaks when I'm stressed; oh, what a luck!
The goldfish watches with a judgy stare,
While I juggle my snacks like I just don't care.

Peeking through curtains, a wild squirrel spies,
His antics remind me of my own silly lies.
The news gets louder, but I just sit still,
With popcorn and giggles, I've had my fill.

Quieted Echoes of Solitude

The walls whisper secrets of what I forgot,
Like that time I wore slippers, but paired with a knot.
My own echo's snort is quite the delight,
It mimics my giggles, then bids me goodnight.

With dust on my shoulders and crumbs on the floor,
I throw a grand party without an encore.
The fridge hums a tune, my dance partner dear,
And I waltz in the kitchen while munching on cheer.

Enfolded in Memories

A blanket of laughter wraps round my soul,
Where socks miss their match, yet still feel whole.
Old photos chuckle, each face knows a jest,
As I sip my tea and consider the quest.

Under a mountain of books yet unread,
I discover my past, where no one's misled.
With giggles and grins, time wraps me in glee,
In the chaos of life, I'm still just in me.

A Cocoon of Reflection

In a room where socks go to hide,
The cat ponders life, with no need to confide.
Pillow forts rise like kingdoms of fluff,
While I sip my tea, saying, 'This is enough!'

Bubble wrap dreams float in the air,
As I dance through my worries, without a care.
My walls are adorned with laughter and cheer,
While my plants hold secrets, but only I hear.

Security in Solitary Spaces

The fridge hums a tune, such a charming sweet song,
While I waddle around, thinking something's gone wrong.

Cheese in one hand, a pickle in tow,
Who needs company? I'm putting on a show!

Climbing the shelves for a snack of pure joy,
Like a curious toddler with a brand-new toy.
My fortress of solitude, a curious scene,
Even the carpet laughs; it's a carpet routine!

Nurtured by the Enclosure

In this nook I create my own personal style,
With goofy décor that can raise a smile.
Teddy bears listen, with wise little grins,
As I tell them my secrets, my losses, my wins.

Tangled in blankets, I'm lost in a maze,
Where every corner whispers my laughter and praise.
The clock ticks away, but it's off on a break,
No deadlines or meetings, just fun's at stake!

Caged Yet Free

A bird in my mind sings, though the cage is quite tight,
While I dance like a lunatic in pajamas at night.
With chips on my shoulders, and crumbs on my chin,
Every jab and every jabber makes me wanna spin!

The walls close in, yet the giggles take flight,
As I zip through this maze, with zeal and delight.
I may be confined, but I've mastered the art,
Of turning these walls into my very own part!

Between the Edges

In a nook where giggles dance,
And socks go missing at first glance,
I found my treasure, a lost remote,
Playing hide and seek with my old coat.

The cat thinks it rules this throne,
While I chase crumbs I once had known,
Laughter echoes in every hall,
Who knew such fun could start so small?

Old boxes filled with tales untold,
Puzzles missing pieces, both bold,
I trip on shoes from days long gone,
This closet life is where I belong!

Outside's a mess of work and fuss,
In here, it's just me, snacks, and us,
So let the world spin on its way,
I'll stay indoors and laugh today!

The Sanctuary of Shadows

In corners dim where whispers creep,
And every pillow's a secret to keep,
A flashlight shines on monster fears,
While laughter hides behind the tears.

The cats plot mischief, oh they scheme,
To steal my snacks, they're on a team,
Dancing shadows move with flair,
In my hideout, I've no time to care.

The dust bunnies gather for a show,
Each one sporting a wild afro,
Seating plans made just for fun,
In this chaos, I am the one!

When daylight fades and dusk draws near,
My kingdom wealthy in joy and cheer,
So let the world toss its heavy rain,
Here, absurdity will always reign!

Closeted Thoughts

In a drawer crammed with dusty dreams,
And half-spilled pots of colorful creams,
I ponder why my socks misalign,
Why all good snacks should taste like pine.

The old sweaters snicker, they know the truth,
Of all the crumbs left from my youth,
A parade of chaos, a disheveled crew,
Plotting adventures from dark to blue.

On paper planes with doodles spun,
I can conquer the universe, oh what fun!
In worlds of whimsy, I take my flight,
With thoughts escaping into the night.

So let the closet keep its charm,
In silly battles, I'll stay warm,
Wrap yourself in stories so grand,
In tangled laughter, life's unplanned!

The Calm of Four Corners

In four corners where silence grins,
And the dust has gathered with all my sins,
A chair reclines, its best years gone,
But in these depths, I'll carry on.

The whims of cushions tell tall tales,
Of pirates, snacks, and mighty gales,
In a fort made of blankets, I conspire,
To face the world amidst laughter's fire.

Who knew a closet could hold such glee?
With every creak, secrets laugh at me,
Lost in the folds of my fortress snug,
Where every monster's just a friendly bug.

So raise a glass to silly schemes,
In corners where reality seems,
To mellow out and bring some cheer,
In my own world—have no fear!

Secure in Timelessness

In a room where socks all vanish,
And dust bunnies plot and plan,
The clock ticks on, a frozen famish,
While I brew tea, a cup in hand.

Cats claim sofas, masters proud,
While I craft snacks with keen delight,
Time flows in a peculiar crowd,
Where minutes stretch into the night.

Singular shirts take on new hues,
Dancing with crumbs, a riotous show,
In a world where old news renews,
And laundry spins as laughter grows.

So here I sit, in cozy trance,
Where echoes giggle in the hall,
In a bubble, no need for a dance,
Content to find my joy in all.

Walls that Soothe the Soul

These walls, they whisper, walls of cheer,
With photos hung, in every nook,
Where echoes of laughter draw so near,
And dust motes dance like a storybook.

They hold my secrets, and my snacks,
And promises made in the hearth's glow,
Each crack a tale of joyful quacks,
Where time slows down, and giggles flow.

A pint of ice cream, a TV show,
A fort of cushions, dreams unfold,
Here's where the hurry seems to slow,
In this embrace, this cozy hold.

So let the world be wild and loud,
I've found my home amidst the jest,
In walls that cradle, soft yet proud,
Nowhere else feels quite like the best.

Wrapped in the Home's Heart

Wrapped in blankets, piles of cheer,
With mismatched socks and stories old,
Here's the place I hold so dear,
Where evenings glimmer, laughter bold.

The fridge hums tunes of midnight treats,
Pizza boxes stacked so high,
In this mess, my heart competes,
For joy that echoes, laughs that fly.

Pajama parties, cozy and bright,
With candles flickering on the brink,
We dawdle and dance to pure delight,
Who needs the world when we just blink?

So here I nest, in this warm embrace,
Where every corner's filled with glee,
In this heart, I've found my place,
A quirky castle, just for me.

The Shelter of Familiarity

In this realm where odd socks thrive,
And cupboards are full of dusty cheer,
The same old chair helps me survive,
With snacks concealed, it draws me near.

Worn-out slippers, my feet's best friends,
Swaying to the rhythm of a show,
Where chaos ends and comfort begins,
And laughter spills, a steady flow.

The echoes of old jokes abide,
With popcorn tossed like grains of sand,
In this shelter, we'll all confide,
Creating memories, hand in hand.

So worry not for what lies outside,
Here's where the fun begins to swell,
In this fortress where love and joy reside,
We find our tales, we weave our spell.

Dreams Behind Sturdy Frames

Within these bounds, I sip my tea,
Daydreaming wildly, a bee carefree.
Walls hold me tight, but I don't mind,
Inventing adventures, with snacks I find.

A pirate's life in the living room,
Dancing with cushions, avoiding the doom.
The cat my crew, we sail through the night,
Wide-open seas, in my pillow fort's light.

The fridge is my treasure, a feast divine,
With every snack, like a rich glass of wine.
I plot my takeover, against the bland chores,
In my fortress of fun, boredom out the doors.

So here I'll stay, with a grin on my face,
Safe in my kingdom, my own little space.
Living like kings, with laughter and games,
Behind sturdy frames, we're all wild and untamed.

Hideaway from the Tempest

The weather outside is a pitiful sight,
But in my nook, everything feels right.
Rain taps the window, a rhythmic sound,
I chuckle and munch on sweets that I've found.

Clouds might be gray, but I'm on a spree,
Building a fortress, just my cat and me.
With books piled high, I claim my throne,
In this glorious chaos, I'm never alone.

Cookies and laughter, who needs the sky?
The storm rages on, but I'm just too spry.
Battling boredom with games and a grin,
A hideaway haven, where no one's a win.

So let the winds howl, let the lightning flash,
Inside my cocoon, I make memories dash.
Each gust a reminder of how fun it feels,
To hideaway from tempests, munching on meals.

Confinement with Comfort

Walls around me, but I don't care,
A fuzzy blanket and comfy chair.
Binging on shows, my senses in flight,
In this snug corner, I feel so right.

Friends on the screen, they laugh and they sing,
Turning my solitude into a king's fling.
Popcorn in hand, a royal delight,
In confinement, I thrive, my future looks bright.

The world may be buzzing, but here it's still,
I dance to my tunes, I swallow each thrill.
Plenty of pillows, I build my own nest,
Convincing myself that I'm truly blessed.

So come, if you must, with a wild chat,
But know I'll be cozy, just like my cat.
This space, oh, so nice, where laughter can bloom,
Confinement with comfort, who needs to zoom?

Embracing the Tightness

In a space so snug, we pile up quite tight,
With friends and laughter, we giggle with might.
Sardines of joy, stuck in this lane,
Counting our blessings, like an honest gain.

The couch is our ship, the cushions our sails,
We navigate life, exchanging old tales.
Stretched like pizza dough, what a fine mess,
Yet in all this chaos, we feel truly blessed.

A heaving heap of old socks and cheer,
As we tell our stories, the world disappears.
Laughter erupts like bubbles in drink,
In this cozy embrace, we don't have to think.

So here's to close quarters, the hugs that we share,
To silly games played in a cozy affair.
Embracing the tightness, we shuffle around,
Strangers no more, in joy we are bound.

Woven Storylines

In a room where socks take flight,
And dust bunnies dance with delight,
Whispers of laughter fill the air,
As chairs conspire in this affair.

The fridge hums tunes like a jazz band,
While spoons are stuck in syrup, unplanned,
Curtains giggle with every breeze,
Where chaos rules, and time just flees.

Cushions plot a playful coup,
Declaring Mondays now taboo,
Cats hold meetings on the sill,
While we are left with laughs to spill.

In this realm of playful fate,
Nothing serious to contemplate,
Beneath the ceiling's cozy glow,
We find the joy in ebb and flow.

Sanctum of Solace

Walls adorned with tales untold,
Of snacks devoured, and naps bold,
The laundry sings a ragged tune,
While chaos sparkles like a boon.

Cups of coffee raise a cheer,
For every spill, a joke appears,
The couch, it sighs, takes on our weight,
As laughter echoes, we feel great.

Shadows play tag with the light,
And every corner hides a slight,
A stash of snacks in every crack,
In this comfort, there's no lack.

The walls may whisper, giggling low,
Holding secrets only they know,
Here, we find our joyful nest,
In our silliness, we are blessed.

Refuge of Remembrance

Here we gather, a motley crew,
With memories deep and laughter too,
Each picture tells a funny tale,
Of mishaps, blunders, never frail.

Mismatched socks, a source of pride,
In this space, we cannot hide,
A treasure trove of silly games,
Where every glitch is worth the claims.

Fruits of labor mashed and tossed,
Leftovers no one cares what's lost,
The clock strikes twelve, and we just grin,
For late-night snacks are where we win.

In this haven, time stands still,
Every chuckle gives a thrill,
And as the walls embrace the sound,
We find our joy forever bound.

Cocooned in Comfort

Pajamas reign in royal flair,
As snacks invade the lazy chair,
Among the pillows, jokes are born,
In this cocoon, the world feels worn.

The walls wear laughter like a cape,
As video games escape the tape,
With each high score, a cheer we share,
In this warm glow, we have no care.

The ceiling fans spin tales so grand,
While dreams of pizza fill the land,
Monsters lurk beneath the bed,
Yet here, we're safe, no need for dread.

With every chuckle, bonds are spun,
In this fortress, we have our fun,
And in this space, we gleefully dwell,
Creating memories all is well.

Safe Havens

In a fortress made of pillows,
The dog claims the throne,
With a crown of snacks piled high,
He's the king, all alone.

In the cupboard, the cookie jar,
Hides treasures oh so sweet,
With sugar-dusted dreams,
We gather for a treat.

Under blankets, we plot and scheme,
For movie nights that glow,
Pajamas worn like armor tight,
Our fortress, all aglow.

The chaos outside may roar and howl,
But here, we never frown,
For laughter fills our fortress walls,
Our kingdom, pajamas brown.

Enclosed Echoes

In the hallway, whispers rise,
Secrets buzz like bees,
My socks a funny alibi,
For sibling escapades, if you please!

Inside these walls, a fortress great,
Echoes of our laughter blend,
Who knew our walls could resonate,
With mischief that won't end?

Potted plants wear funny hats,
A cactus pricks at dawn,
Yet in this quirky castle space,
An army of houseplants spawn.

With every creak and crack they make,
Our secrets intertwine,
In echoes of a giggled fate,
A fortress by design.

Secrets Behind Closed Doors

Behind the door, a stash of joy,
My crayons and a map,
Where pirates sail and toys deploy,
In a world where I can nap.

A closet filled with costumes bright,
A superhero in disguise,
With capes that shine like stars at night,
Adventure's in our eyes.

Whispers dance like fireflies,
In corners where we scheme,
A treasure hunt, a sock surprise,
Find the lost pair—what a dream!

Giggles spill like bubblegum,
In these rooms, it's fun galore,
Behind the door, a world so dumb,
Adventure forevermore!

Stronghold of Solitude

In my room, the fortress stands,
   Guarded by a messy floor,
My fortress built with Lego hands,
   Where no adults explore.

A stronghold made of comic books,
   With snacks stacked to the sky,
Here, I'm safe from pesky looks,
   As I munch and wave goodbye.

The world outside can spin and sway,
   But there's magic in my space,
With every clumsy move I play,
   I find my happy place.

Each giggle echoes, walls absorb,
   My laughter fills the hall,
In this realm that I adore,
   I reign, the ruler of it all.

Between the Beams

A mouse wore shoes made of cheese,
He danced on beams with such great ease.
The cat looked on, quite perplexed,
Thinking of dinner, feeling vexed.

The spider spun silk like a pro,
While ants formed a marching row.
The broom came close, chaos would reign,
But laughter echoed, easing the pain.

A gnome tucked in with his hat askew,
Claimed he'd found a treasure or two.
Turns out it was just dust and fluff,
Still, he claimed it was quite enough.

So here we are, a merry crew,
Behind walls that make mischief brew.
With giggles trapped in every crack,
We'll party hard, no looking back.

Fortress of Dreams

A knight tried hard to impress the queen,
But kept tripping over his own sheen.
He polished his armor until it gleamed,
But forgot his sword; was he really deemed?

In the courtyard, dragons roamed around,
All were clucking, hardly profound.
They huffed and puffed, with fire and flair,
Yet all they did was style their hair.

With pillows stacked up like a tower,
The jester tried to rap, absurd and dour.
He slipped on a beetle and fell with a thud,
Yet laughed it off, 'It's just a mud!'

The castle rang with raucous cheer,
As dreams unwound, and mishaps steered.
In this fortress where laughter was plenty,
Who needed battles? Life felt so zany!

Interwoven Lives

Two cats and a dog shared a space,
One wore glasses, looking quite ace.
They plotted schemes to steal some food,
While a parrot squawked, 'Get in the mood!'

The goldfish swam with graceful flair,
They thought he'd join them for a share.
But he just flipped, bubbles escaping,
Said, 'You folks? I'm not mis-shaping!'

A bat hung upside-down, taking a nap,
The dogs barked loud—oh, what a trap!
He woke in a flap and spread his wings,
'What's all this ruckus? Can't a bat swing?'

In this circus of laughter and cheer,
Where pets made life bright with no space for fear,
The walls held secrets in stitches and winks,
A bond so rich that it rarely shrinks.

The Cloistered Haven

In a nook where oddballs dared to play,
A hedgehog planned a wild soiree.
He donned a tutu, feeling quite grand,
With disco lights set up by a band.

The birds sang off-key, but with such pride,
The turtle danced slow, taking it in stride.
While the frogs all croaked, managing tones,
Caught up in the music, lost in their zones.

A squirrel slipped nut snacks, with glee,
Yelled, 'More for me, come one, come three!'
But all the while, he bumbled about,
Creating a ruckus, without a doubt.

In this haven, where odd meets the quirky,
Life was a show, never murky.
With laughter pouring like sweet lemonade,
These cloistered creatures never afraid.

The Protective Embrace of Stone

Inside these sturdy realms we stay,
Where echoes bounce and laugh all day.
The walls may seem quite rough and tough,
But here we find our cozy fluff.

With every thud and playful sound,
A bouncing ball reveals the ground.
We dodge the corners, swing the door,
For who would tease the stone's apparel?

Hiding from the world outside,
Within these stones, our giggles slide.
The doorbell's ding is just for fun,
We answer with a rubber bun.

Oh how the walls have seen our plays,
As we enact our silly displays.
While neighbors wonder, laugh we must,
In our embrace, we find the trust.

Quietude Behind Bars

Behind this cage of bars, we grin,
Where laughter hums and tails spin.
The world outside may seem quite bleak,
But here, we play hide and seek.

Each clink and clang, a soothing song,
As we dance and tumble along.
The silence wraps like velvet soft,
In this fortress, we take off!

Though strangers squint and scratch their heads,
We gather here, dream on our beds.
With every peek and goofy pose,
We bear our joys like garden grows.

Sometimes it feels like a circus ring,
As we juggle thoughts and chat and sing.
So let them watch, we're quite the sight,
Finding joy in our quaint little plight.

The Layers of Tranquility

Built of layers, one on the other,
Each layer whispers, "There's no bother."
We pile our thoughts like frosty snow,
Crafting dreams in the dance of flow.

With silly hats and mismatched socks,
We craft our joy, we dodge the clocks.
Each layer thickens with a smile,
Who said we can't be free a while?

The world outside can stomp and frown,
But here we twirl, we wear the crown.
Beneath the warmth, we laugh and play,
In layered joys, we find our way.

So let the winds howl all they want,
We've got our plans, our silly jaunt.
As layers twine and echo dance,
We in our fortress, take a chance.

Inward Whispers of Warmth

Whispers flutter like butterflies,
In the heart's core, where laughter lies.
Inward dreams in corners deep,
We find the secrets that we keep.

With every chuckle, walls respond,
A secret handshake, a magic bond.
Silly tales unfurl like streams,
While the outside world just schemes.

Behind the curtains, shadows play,
We sprinkle joy like confetti spray.
Inward echoes, soft and light,
Turn ordinary into delight.

So hang the lights and pop the corn,
In our retreat, we'll laugh till morn.
For every path leads back to glee,
In our warm cocoon, we're wild and free.

Comfort of the Tightly Bound

In cozy corners, we do reside,
With snacks piled high, our secret pride.
The world outside can surely wait,
As we debate on pizza fate.

The curtains drawn, we laugh and play,
In our little nook, we choose to stay.
A raucous game of hide and seek,
Unless the cat decides to peek.

Our laughter echoes, walls embrace,
No need for pants, just stay in place.
With pillows stacked like fortress walls,
We conquer kingdoms, heed our calls.

No pizza delivery can withstand,
The power of our snack-filled land.
In giggles wrapped, we'll always find,
The joy that's ours, the fun aligned.

Inside the Embrace of Isolation

In our little bubble, snug and tight,
We watch reruns, our hearts take flight.
The outside world? It sounds quite bleak,
But here, the snacks are always peak.

Calendar reminders serve no aim,
Every day's a glorious game.
In fuzzy socks, we twirl and spin,
Our dance-off makes the neighbors grin.

With every sigh, a giggle will bloom,
Who knew together we'd fill the room?
Reading novels upside down,
In our fortress, we wear the crown.

Though walls surround, they cannot confine,
Our wild imaginations intertwine.
We build great dreams with jumbled plans,
And conquer worlds with silly bans.

The Serenity of Limitations

Within these walls, our world is grand,
Limited views, but fun is planned.
We tame our boredom, with a game or two,
In this seven-day twilight hue.

No need for fancy, bustling malls,
We shop for joy within these walls.
The fridge becomes our city square,
Where culinary dreams fill the air.

The world outside can fret and fume,
But here together, we forever bloom.
With coffee spills and laughter loud,
We thrive, a merry, goofy crowd.

Through limited ways, our tales are spun,
In pajama days, we still have fun.
Together here, the spirit lifts,
And finds delight in simple gifts.

The Embrace Beyond the Frame

In frames that hold our silly faces,
We capture joy in lesser places.
Every cringe and blooper caught,
A tapestry of laughter wrought.

Painted walls, misfit decor,
Our style is grand—who needs much more?
The cushions hold our dreams and thoughts,
In this realm, we're always caught.

With crafty hands, our art displayed,
Bright neon colors, a world remade.
Outside the lines, we color free,
In this embrace, we're meant to be.

As sunsets paint the frames anew,
We tip our hats to every hue.
In this odd place, a home so bright,
We've found our bliss, our heart's delight.

The Walls That Hold Us

In laundry rooms, I lose my socks,
The walls conspire, oh what a shock.
They giggle softly, hide my shoes,
A funny dance in plaid and blues.

Behind the couch, the dust bunnies play,
Making shadows that seem to sway.
They throw a party when I'm not around,
With crumbs and laughter scattered on the ground.

The kitchen sings with pots and pans,
A symphony of spoons and cans.
The fridge hums jokes in chilled delight,
As we gather 'round each cozy night.

Even the walls have stories to tell,
About socks and snacks that fell.
In every crack, a chuckle lives,
A funny home that always gives.

Silent Company of the Enclosed

Behind my door, a riot brews,
The walls whisper tales of lost shoes.
In silent mirth, they hold good cheer,
With every creak, they draw me near.

Under the stairs, a cat does lurk,
Plotting mischief with a quirky smirk.
He nods to walls that keep him safe,
In our quaint little space, he's king of the waif.

The kitchen clock ticks a clever rhyme,
Measuring leftovers, keeping time.
While plates and spoons engage in chat,
With a wink and nudge from the old floor mat.

Walls that hold laughter, keep hearts bold,
In secret recesses, stories unfold.
They share our blunders, our goofy tricks,
So trust these bounds, they're all in the mix.

The Heartbeat of Home

In corners lurk, the echoes of glee,
Where laughter bounces, wild and free.
The heart of home beats in rhythm and song,
With quirks and giggles, we all belong.

Under the table, the dog dreams wide,
Chasing shadows, taking a ride.
The walls listen close, with a knowing grin,
As every chuckle sinks deep within.

Fridge magnets shuffle in playful cheer,
Spell out words that tickle the ear.
On rainy days, we shimmy and shake,
While walls hold tight, no chance to break.

So here we are, in our joyful space,
With laughter woven, a playful lace.
Old photos giggle from the mantel's top,
As the heartbeat of home won't ever stop.

Interiors of Peace

Behind closed doors, the world is still,
Where jokes take flight, and laughter spills.
A chaos wrapped in a gentle hug,
As pillows doodle, all snug as a bug.

The coffee pot gurgles a happy tune,
Echoing vibes of a friendly afternoon.
While chairs spin tales of old and new,
In spaces that hold what we cherish too.

The curtains nod in a breezy dance,
While socks do a jig, given the chance.
Walls whisper secrets, a soft serenade,
In these restful corners, we've joyfully laid.

So let's toast to the quirks of our place,
The funny moments we lovingly trace.
With each room holding the gift of delight,
Our interiors of peace take off in flight.

The Coziness of Containment

In a tiny room where socks conspire,
Piles of laundry reach all the way higher.
Couches whisper secrets to the wall,
While hidden snacks await for a midnight call.

Pots and pans dance a clumsy jig,
A rogue spoon leaps and does a big gig.
Cats form a union on my big chair,
Declaring their rule with a feline glare.

Walls tickle my thoughts in cozy embrace,
While the dust bunnies race in their little space.
TV laughs and echoes throughout the day,
As I chuckle at life's clumsy ballet.

In this fortress of fluff, where quirks are keen,
Every corner sings of a silly routine.
Life's a series of giggles, none too tall,
In this snug little kingdom, I'm having a ball.

Enclosure of the Mind

Behind the curtain of my thought parade,
Ideas frolic, never planned or made.
Tangled neurons in comical fights,
Deciding if daydreams or snacks take flight.

My brain's a circus, with clowns in a row,
Juggling tasks, while the popcorn does grow.
Contemplating dinner or a silly rhyme,
Both flavors seem tasty, I'm out of time.

Thoughts waltz around in a quirky spree,
Chasing wild whims like they're chasing me.
Every odd notion clinks like a bell,
Spilling laughter that only I can tell.

In my mental room where antics unfold,
Each silly sentiment feels warm and bold.
Here I find joy in the swirling grind,
A fabulous frenzy, the best of its kind.

A Safe Harbor of Thought

In a pocket of thoughts, where giggles abide,
The vessels of laughter drift with the tide.
Silly ideas like ducks in a row,
Paddle around in the mind's little show.

A boat made of dreams sails on a whim,
Catching the breeze from a cozy brim.
Witty reflections dance like a game,
Of tag with my mind that can never be tamed.

Each wave of nonsense splashes with cheer,
In this harbor of humor, there's nothing to fear.
Thoughts twirl like fish, in a slapstick play,
Bubbling with joy as they frolic away.

Here in this cove, where safety's a flip,
I dip into laughter on each silly trip.
Anchored in whimsy, I drift and I glide,
In this delightful haven, I'll always reside.

Protecting the Inner Light

Within these walls, where giggles softly glow,
I guard my humor like a radiant show.
Lighthearted musings float like balloons,
As I juggle my thoughts with silly tunes.

A lighthouse of laughter beams through the cracks,
Guiding lost hopes back from their tracks.
Each chuckle a wave, and each grin a sail,
Charting the course for the comical trail.

In this fortress of joy, where mirth takes flight,
Every shadow dances, inspired by light.
I create a bubble where sunshine can peek,
As I laugh through the days and the moments unique.

So come join the giggles, let worries take flight,
In this chamber of cheer, all's effortlessly bright.
Together we'll shine, in our whimsical plight,
Protecting the essence of pure, silly light.

Secure Moments on the Inside

In a fortress made of snack packs,
We hide from world's loud claps.
Chips crunch as we giggle bright,
Dancing shadows in the pale moonlight.

Pillows stacked like a castle high,
We plot to skip, oh my, oh my!
Sipping soda, hearts take flight,
In our kingdom, all feels right.

The cat's our knight in fuzzy coat,
He guards our dreams as we gloat.
Netflix plays, our laughter rings,
Here's where joy forever clings.

From the couch, we rule our zone,
No place like home, or on the throne.
When life gets tough, we shout, "Hooray!"
Cocooned bliss is here to stay.

The Warmth of the Encompassing

Fluffy blankets draped like clouds,
In our realm, we're laughing loud.
We sip on cocoa, marshmallow fluff,
The outside can be way too tough.

With board games stacked like a tower tall,
We conquer lands, we never fall.
Giggles echo through our lair,
Who needs fresh air? We don't care!

Anarchy reigns with silly hats,
While plotting pranks on the chubby cat.
Each tickle fight laughs off stress,
Inside this haven, we've found success.

Secrets shared in candlelight,
A cozy circle, oh what a sight!
With chocolate bars and bear hugs tight,
Our fortress bubbles with pure delight.

Residing in the Gentle Grip

Nestled in a sea of socks,
Brushing off the ticking clocks.
In pajamas worn for days on end,
We laugh and play, who needs a trend?

Crayons and doodles cover the floor,
With masterpieces we truly adore.
Moments spark with a funny sound,
In our safe place, joy abounds.

Funny faces on ice cream jars,
We toast to life beneath the stars.
Each joke traded, a treasure sweet,
The sparkle of life feels so complete.

With the world outside in a fray,
We mix up absurd games to play.
In laughter's arms, we find our bliss,
Every moment wrapped in this warm kiss.

Life Behind the Safe Facade

Behind the door, our giggles soar,
Who knew home could be such a roar?
With pizza slices, toppings galore,
We munch and crunch, always wanting more.

A blanket fort reaches the ceiling high,
Where dreams are spun, and we just fly.
Each corner holds a laugh or two,
In our snug space, there's so much to do.

Odd socks dance in a funny line,
Here in our bubble, everything's fine.
The outside lets slips of serious fun,
But here we thrive, oh yes, we run!

So cheers to moments behind the mask,
Who needs to play when inside's the task?
Where friendship's woven with tasty bars,
In our world, we're the shining stars!

The Shield of Solitude

Inside my fort, I munch on snacks,
While laughing at the world outside,
My cat believes he leads the pack,
As I take a break from the daily grind.

Pajamas my armor, no judging here,
I dance like nobody's watching me,
The mirror laughs, but I have no fear,
In this joyous bubble, I'm wild and free.

With a pillow for a trusty sword,
I duel with boredom, but I won each time,
The walls echo my laughter adored,
Creating a canvas for my silly rhyme.

So bring on the chaos of workday news,
I'll be here chuckling, safe from strife,
In this humorous space, I pay my dues,
Where giggles wage war against the mundane life.

The Haven of Heart's Whispers

Here in my nook, where whispers play,
I share secrets with my teacup friend,
Each sip a story, in a merry ballet,
That never seems to want to end.

The walls wear pictures of laughter and cheer,
Like confetti, they circle my head,
In this jovial maze, nothing's unclear,
As I dodge reality, my worries fled.

Doodling my dreams with colorful pens,
While my socks are mismatched, but who really cares?
A dance with the dust bunnies, that never ends,
We laugh at the plight of our very own lairs.

In this haven of giggles, all's right as rain,
The outside can wait, let them stew in their grind,
With each playful moment, I dance without pain,
In this delightful retreat, my joy I find.

Engulfed in Gentle Echoes

In the cocoon of my fluffy chair,
I float away on my comic book cloud,
With echoes of laughter filling the air,
And silly thoughts that make me proud.

My socks, they wage a colorful strike,
While I concoct schemes just to be silly,
I giggle aloud, oh what a delight,
In this cuddly kingdom, I reign willy-nilly.

Cooking up mischief with kitchen gloves,
The spatula dances, my partner in crime,
As cupcakes giggle and whisper of love,
In this echo chamber, we share our prime.

Here's to the moments, the chuckles we glean,
Inside these walls, where time loses pace,
For laughter's the treasure, bright and serene,
In my cozy retreat, I find my place.

In the Embrace of Safe Space

Nestled within my blanket cocoon,
I'm plotting a coup against Monday's dread,
With snacks as my army, they'll croon a tune,
Of joy and delight danced out of bed.

Tickles and giggles take up the space,
As I twirl like a ballerina of quirks,
The pets join the ballet, all clueless and grace,
And we giggle together, a troupe that works.

With cushions for walls, I feel so grand,
Forming a fortress against the day's chase,
The laughter erupts, like it had been planned,
In this quirky bastion, joy finds its place.

So here's to the silly and moments we keep,
In invisible armor, away from the race,
In this laughter-filled land, my heart takes a leap,
Creating a world wrapped in gentle embrace.

Cocooned in Protective Layers

In my fortress made of cushions,
I'm the king of all distractions.
Pillows piled like mighty mountains,
Naptime calls with grand attractions.

My snacks are stacked, a tasty wall,
Guarded fiercely, don't you dare!
Invisible moat, a couch to sprawl,
Friends can visit, but snacks? Beware!

I wear my blanket like a cape,
Hero of this cozy land.
Every sneeze becomes an escape,
Against life's chaos, we take a stand.

So let the world outside go wild,
I reign from my plushy haven.
Childlike laughter, the heart of a child,
In my fortress, I'm always craven.

Outside, the World Stirs

The sun is bright, a ball of fluff,
But I'm busy with my trinkets.
Outside's rumored to be tough,
I'll just stay here with my sphinxes.

Birds are chirping, chips are crunching,
The trees are dancing, oh how rude!
From my fortress, I'm just munching,
With my blanket fort attitude.

Someone knocks, it's Auntie Sue,
Her jokes fly like a thousand bees.
I smile, wave, and shout "Not you!"
I'll stay put, with my PJs and cheese.

Oh, outside's vibrant, full of thrill,
But dear friend, I'm just too chill.
This bubble wraps my laughter tight,
Adventure can wait for another night!

The Secret Garden of Security

Behind my door, a realm unique,
Where dust bunnies perform ballet.
In a world of socks, I sneak,
A kingdom of snacks on display.

Plants are thriving, books are stacked,
My magic realm, a treasure trove.
Here, no troubles can be attacked,
Only giggles and blankets to stow.

Sunflowers wave, in silence they giggle,
While my cat plots the great escape.
I now control the daily wiggle,
In this fortress, I overwatch the landscape.

And if the mailman makes a scene,
With parcels loud and hefty cheer,
I'll take a bow, a hidden queen,
In my secret garden, I shift in gear.

A Retreat from the Storm

As thunder claps like a snoring bear,
I hunker down with my hot tea.
Clouds might glare with a lightning stare,
Like nature's movie, free entry.

With snacks galore strewn about my floor,
I've built a fort from these fluffy pillows.
Rain drops tap on the window's door,
While I dance with ferocious jell-o.

Fortifications made from laughter and crumbs,
A high-tech contraption of whimsy and glee.
Outside, the chaos thunders and hums,
But in here, I'm as happy as can be.

So let the storm sing its loud tune,
I've got games and giggles galore.
In this haven, I'll sway like the moon,
Until the bright sun shines once more.

Within the Comforting Embrace

Beneath the roof where socks go missing,
Cats play cards, the dog is hissing.
Dust bunnies dance in a waltz so bright,
While my favorite snack is lost from sight.

Lampshades wear hats, they think they're grand,
With mismatched socks, it's quite the band.
The fridge sings tunes gone slightly sour,
As I chase the cat for an hour's power.

Chairs hold secrets in their soft embrace,
Each creak and groan shares a funny face.
Television mutters, the remote's in a fray,
Yet laughter echoes in a silly ballet.

So here I sit, in a whirl of cheer,
With my quirky friends, I have no fear.
Inside these walls, the joy unfolds,
In this haven of happiness, life never gets old.

The Sanctuary of Heartfelt Thoughts

In a realm of mismatched socks and dishes,
Dreams take flight, granting all my wishes.
The teapot whistles a silly song,
While my goldfish judges me, all day long.

Walls hum tunes with a gentle sway,
As pictures gossip in their own display.
The couch is a ship sailing on a sea,
Of popcorn and crumbs, it belongs to me.

Books lean in, sharing tales quite tall,
While my slippers plot their escape from the hall.
Clocks spin around, they're stuck in a race,
Tick-tock giggles fill the empty space.

So here in this haven of whimsical cheer,
Every mischief and memory brings me near.
Each lighthearted moment, a piece of art,
In this sanctuary of my happy heart.

Anchored in Familiar Surroundings

In this cozy nook where the ceiling squeaks,
I find my peace amidst giggles and leaks.
The toaster pops toast like a surprise,
While my plant gives me those judgmental eyes.

The fridge hums jokes no one understands,
As pen pensively writes on unturned lands.
Socks argue loudly about their pair,
While the cat just yawns, without a care.

The couch offers comfort like a soft clout,
As I plot my escape from the daily rout.
In corners abound with secrets and dust,
Every hiccup of laughter is a joyful must.

So let's raise a glass to this merry space,
Where every quirk has its own lovely place.
Anchored in joy, with a giggle or two,
In familiar surroundings, I thrive anew.

Peace in Every Corner

In each quiet nook, a nightlight grins,
With mismatched spoons having their spins.
Chairs conspire as the curtains sway,
Whispering dreams of a sleepy ballet.

The rug tells tales of the shoes it has known,
Of muddy paws and seeds that were sown.
Each shadow flutters with a playful tease,
As my worries dissolve like a sweet summer breeze.

Painting debates about colors it should,
While I munch popcorn for some tasty good.
The clock spins tales of moments we steal,
In the warmth of the space, all worries repeal.

Here in this haven where laughter can bloom,
Every corner whispers of joys to consume.
Finding peace in the chaos that comes and goes,
In the dance of my thoughts, how laughter grows.

Bound by Timeless Strains

In this abode of misfit socks,
The fridge is filled with odd phone docks.
The cat walks on the dining table,
Where peasants feast on dry dog label.

The walls are painted with jokes and glee,
Where laughter echoes, wild and free.
We dance like fools in mismatched shoes,
And argue over whose turn to snooze.

The decor's a clash, a splendid mess,
With haphazard art and love's caress.
Couch cushions are castles, cushions are crowns,
Yet, here we grumble, not frowns, only crowns.

In this place where chaos reigns supreme,
We bask in the glory of the hilarity dream.
Every clang and clash is a giggly song,
In our quirky lair, how could anything be wrong?

Nest of Tranquility

In this cozy nook, we nest and squabble,
With pillows soft, never loveable trouble.
The remote control gets lost in the fray,
It's always the same, come what may.

Inside this haven, where silence can snore,
Sneaky snacks hide behind the kitchen door.
Whispers are muffled like secrets in fog,
We giggle at echoes of probing old dogs.

The dust bunnies dance in the warm moonlight,
As squirrels outside take their evening flight.
With cookies that crumbled and stories quite tall,
We feast on the laughter; it's fun after all.

Wrapped in our layers, all cozy and bright,
With shenanigans done by the stars at night.
This nest of peace has comedic flair,
Like socks on the roof, it's quite a rare affair!

Hidden in Sanctuary Shadows

In corners where shadows stretch and yawn,
The dog snorts like thunder, an endless dawn.
Behind the couch, old treasures reside,
Like popcorn kernels and lost jokes, all tried.

The windows creak stories of raindrops past,
While the cat spins tales, oh, what a blast!
With giggles that bounce off the dusty old books,
Our sanctuary laughs in all kinds of hooks.

We slapstick around, our dance is absurd,
A chorus of chaos, not a whisper heard.
From the fridge comes a thump, is it cheese gone rogue?
Or just my sneaky roommate, playing the hog?

In shadows, we find our cackling delight,
As crickets cheer us in the moonlit night.
This patchwork of whimsy, a castle of jest,
In a world of bright nonsense, we're truly blessed!

Embracing the Silence

In our fortress of giggles, silence isn't loud,
We whisper our secrets beneath the cloud.
Where silence wraps round like a warm fuzzy hug,
And the vacuum cleaner is our mischievous bug.

With blankets galore, we build our retreat,
From the slightest of movements, our hearts skip a beat.
The dishes may pile, though dishes we dread,
Our laughter erupts over crumbs on the bed.

In the stillness, we map out our dreams,
Beneath layers of laughter, life's giggles it seems.
Echoes of fun bounce off fridge and wall,
In this sweet sanctuary, we stumble and sprawl.

So embrace all the silence, we welcome the jest,
As the world spins away, we're simply the best.
With snorts and chuckles that light up the gloom,
In our treasured expanse, chaos finds room!

Behind the Guardian's Gaze

In a fortress tall, watch the guards admire,
With their shiny steel hats, they look so dire.
Lifting their swords like they're stuck in a pose,
While birds make their nests right beneath their nose.

Underneath the ramparts, the jester takes flight,
Telling tales of dragons that don't bite at night.
The guards roll their eyes, but the jesters all cackle,
In this kingdom where jokes are the greatest of battles.

With catapults ready, they'll fling all the puns,
Beyond those high walls, just wait for the runs.
A tickle attack from the towers above,
Where laughter and gags are the softest of love.

When the sun sets low, they dance near the moat,
Making merry and mirth as they clamber and gloat.
Who knew that a castle could hold such delight?
Behind the gaze of the guards, the fun takes flight!

Embraced by Brick and Mortar

In the heart of the castle, where the bricks are tight,
A party of squirrels is planning tonight.
With acorns for snacks and a treasure map,
They're hosting a feast, where no one will nap.

The knights in the tower pretend to be tough,
But peek through the window – they're playing with fluff.

With bright-colored yarn and their helmets askew,
Those warriors of yore are now weaving a zoo.

The walls whisper secrets, a giggle or two,
As the jesters perform their routine, quite new.
Dancing and prancing on cobblestone floors,
While the guards scratch their heads, confused by the roars.

As night drapes the castle in shadows so deep,
The laughter erupts, making all of it leap.
In this brickwork embrace, oh, what a delight,
Where joy finds its way, like a firefly's flight!

Whispered Walls

The whispers in corridors, oh how they tease,
Like a playful breeze rustling the leaves.
"Did you see that knight trip over his shoe?"
The walls chuckle softly, yes, they know too!

At dusk, when the candles flicker and sway,
The bricks tell of chaos from many a day.
Of knights who've misstepped and ladies who snort,
Their stories, quite comical, become the retort.

With echoes of laughter that bounce down the hall,
Those stones hold the essence of each funny fall.
Sitting in corners, the ghosts share their views,
On the antics of folks, and their outlandish shoes.

So gather your friends, bring a joke or two,
As the walls will expound on their humors anew.
In the glow of the moon, under starry heights,
Let the whispered walls laugh through the long, jovial nights!

The Heart's Fortress

Behind the stout gates where the brave often tread,
Lies a heart full of laughter, not sorrow or dread.
The jesters, they march, with a bounce in their step,
While kings and their crowns silently wept.

The heart holds a secret, a stash full of fun,
With whoopee cushions hidden for everyone.
When the jester says "Boo!" with a flick of his bow,
The knights and the ladies erupt in a "Oh!"

From banquets of pudding with sprinkles galore,
To pie fights that spill through the grand castle door.
Each room's a new stage for mischief and play,
In the heart of this fortress, fun leads the way.

So come, take a peek at this castle's true art,
Where jesters and laughter just never depart.
In this heart made of giggles, let all worries cease,
For within these bright walls, we find sheerest peace!

Strength in the Surrounding Barriers

My cat thinks he's a lion, oh what a sight,
On the couch he defends us, ready to fight.
With a flick of his tail and a noble pose,
He guards our kingdom while napping, who knows?

The dog plays bouncer, barking at the door,
He jumps like a kangaroo, always wanting more.
With treats in hand, they form quite the clan,
Laughing at shadows, as only they can.

Our fridge is a fortress, filled to the brim,
With snacks that we nibble on, life's not so grim.
We build up the walls, with laughter and cheers,
In this cozy haven, we conquer our fears.

So here in our bubble, the outside's a slog,
We're safe from the world, like a dog on a log.
With a wink and a smile, we dance through the night,
In barriers of laughter, everything's right!

Within the Boundaries

With crayons and markers, we color our space,
Doodles of joy, each one has a face.
The dog guards the crayons, he thinks they're a treat,
Stealing the show (and the cheese snacks) is neat!

Fortresses built with cushions piled high,
As we launch paper planes that soar through the sky.
Mom yells from the kitchen, the TV's too loud,
But laughter echoes, we're one happy crowd.

Pajama parties with movies galore,
Popcorn explosions, we settle for more.
The walls hear our secrets, our snickers, our schemes,
In this realm of mischief, we live out our dreams.

Our home is a playground, where all things collide,
Adventure awaits, with laughter our guide.
With giggles and games, we banish the gray,
Within our own bubble, we're happy to play!

Echoes of Safety

Inside these four walls, we play hide and seek,
In cramped little corners, we laugh and squeak.
The cat peeks around with a curious stare,
A surprise ambush always leads to a scare!

We wrap ourselves tight in a blanket cocoon,
Imagining kings and queens, we'll find our own moon.
With sippy cups raised, we toast to the night,
As bubbles of laughter shimmer in flight.

The door may be locked, but our minds wander free,
Across jungles of pillows, oh, what a spree!
Every shadow a pirate, every noise is a ghost,
Yet within our own walls, we're proud of our boast.

So here we will giggle and whisper our dreams,
In echoes of safety, life isn't as it seems.
With love all around, and snacks to devour,
Our castle stands tall, the fun's in full power!

Refuge from the Chaos

In a world full of noise, we find our own beat,
With the TV on blast, let the chaos retreat.
The laundry piles high like a mountain's great crest,
But we're kings and queens in our friendly unrest.

Our fortress of cushions is fit for a throne,
With teddy bears standing guard, never alone.
We declare silly wars, tickle attacks roam,
In this glorious madness, we find our sweet home.

A cookie jar stands like a shimmering prize,
The secret to joy is a snack in disguise.
With tummy aches laughing, we chomp 'til we're full,
In this refuge from chaos, life's no longer dull.

So let the world spin, let the wind roar,
Here in our hideout, there's always much more.
With joy in our hearts, we'll dance through it all,
In our funny little haven, we'll never let fall!

The Enclosed Realm

In a room filled with socks, and a cat on a chair,
Beneath a fortress of crumbs, we giggle and share.
The walls, they seem thick, like a pastry delight,
Yet they echo the laughter that woos in the night.

With each little thud, my heart does a dance,
As cupboards hold secrets of the great snack romance.
A chair's a throne made of fluff and of dreams,
In our kingdom of chaos, life's never what it seems.

The light from the window casts shadows so grand,
While we tiptoe through laughter, a curious band.
In our little domain, oh the joy we create,
With a wink and a chuckle, we dash past the gate.

From our private abode, we cast out our spells,
Built from the stories that nobody tells.
So raise up your glass, to the giggles we find,
In our quirky abode, may the world be unlined.

Veils of Protection

Behind four sturdy walls, life's a comic display,
As dust bunnies tumble in a whimsical way.
The couch is a mountain, the pillows our friends,
In this merry domain, the fun never ends.

Thick carpets of laughter, where secret things grow,
Like a garden of weirdness, it's all for the show.
We barter for snacks, while the TV's a spy,
Plotting our future like a pie in the sky.

The kitchen's a dance floor, pots twirl with delight,
While I flip a pancake into marvelous flight.
The fridge is a vault, where treasures reside,
In this hidden abyss, even veggies can't hide.

While echoes of chatter bounce off of the frames,
Each cackle a victory, each giggle a game.
Here, adventure collides with the hum of the day,
In our safe little bubble, we laugh all the way.

Cradled by Structure

Within these four corners, comedies brew,
As shadows dance jigs and the clock laughs too.
We're the rulers of nonsense, our scepter a spoon,
In this land of absurd, we outshine the moon.

Pajamas our armor, we venture each night,
On quests for lost socks, oh what a sight!
The floor is a jungle, and cushions the trees,
In this fortress of laughter, we're never at ease.

Cupboards hold treasures, like candy and cheer,
While echoes of madness fill each happy sphere.
With giggles like fireworks lighting the dark,
We're the jesters of joy, leaving trails of a spark.

So here's to our haven, a sanctuary grand,
Where fun chases mischief, hand in hand.
Amid the wild whimsy, we always will roam,
In our cherished cocoon, forever our home.

The Quiet Enclave

In corners quite cozy, where whispers abound,
Lies a realm of peculiar, a magical ground.
Mugs filled with giggles, that spill on the floor,
In this nook of delight, we're never a bore.

The walls wear their paint like a cloak of the past,
While shadows insist that our fun must last.
With every loud snicker, a memory grows,
In a place where absurdity endlessly flows.

As chairs wobble gently, we spin tales that flare,
Of dragons and dungeons, and times we all dare.
Beneath blankets of laughter, dreams weave through the air,
In this tiny enclosure, we dance without care.

So smile through the chaos, let worry take flight,
For in this small refuge, we shine ever bright.
With humor as our armor, we can't help but cheer,
In this quiet enclave, we've nothing to fear.

The Haven Behind Closed Doors

In a world of socks and mismatched shoes,
I hide from chores, I've got nothing to lose.
The fridge is glowing, a beacon of hope,
While dust bunnies dance, oh how they elope.

Neighbors peep in, with their prying eyes,
They think I'm a hermit, or wearing a disguise.
But inside these walls, it's a grand masquerade,
With snacks in my lap, my worries will fade.

My cat is the queen, she rules with a paw,
A sassy meow, not a hint of a flaw.
We throw our own parties, just she and I,
With popcorn confetti, we dance 'til we sigh.

So if you drop by, no need for a ruckus,
We'll film the next blockbuster, starring my tusks!
In the haven behind closed doors, we'll play,
Where laughter and snacks always win the day.

Enclosed by an Embrace

In this snug little nook, where my pillow takes flight,
I cackle at sitcoms that run through the night.
My blanket's my sidekick, a cozy best friend,
With popcorn on deck, let the chuckles extend.

I try to bake cookies, they spread like a blob,
A baking disaster, but I cannot sob.
The smoke alarms sing, like a chorus so sweet,
With treats made of chaos, I call it a feat!

I'd step out for a jog, but my couch has me hooked,
It whispers such secrets that have me quite booked.
I'm building a fort from the clothes on my chair,
It's an epic domain—no one else needs to care.

So here in my fortress, I chuckle with glee,
In the embrace of these walls, I'm as happy as can be!
The outside can wait, let it rain or it shine,
For the fun never ends in this world that's all mine.

Comfort in the Shadows

In the dim light of corners, where mischief takes flight,
I twirl with my shadows, all giggles and light.
Chasing dust motes like fireflies on a spree,
In the nooks of my fortress, there's laughter with glee.

Cuddled up tight with snacks piled so high,
My spirit takes wing, as the sitcoms fly by.
With a remote as my scepter, I reign in delight,
Each episode richer, each couch cushion bright.

The walls may be quiet, but inside I'm a dreamer,
Inventing grand schemes, an imaginary schemer.
I'm king of the castle, though it's made from a bed,
With laughter and crumbs, I'm a ruler well-fed.

When friends knock on my door, with smiles and good cheer,
I'll welcome them in, for the fun draws them near.
But the moment they leave, back to shadows I leap,
For the comfort of solitude's where I find sheep.

Fortress of Solace

In my fortress of solace, I giggle and roam,
With walls like a hug, I can chill at home.
I've got games on the shelf, a throne made of snacks,
Where I'm queen of the couch, and there's no need for hacks.

Boredom's a myth, in my castle so grand,
I spin epic tales from the stuff that I've planned.
In the quiet of corners, I plot and I scheme,
A master of chaos, a laughter machine.

The fridge is my counsel, my loyal advisor,
With leftover wisdom that makes me a riser.
Each wobble of dance as I fetch my next treat,
Is a fierce declaration that I'm living elite.

So come join my kingdom, where humor's the flag,
With giggles as banners, you'll never feel drab.
In this fortress of solace, we'll laugh through the night,
Where each silly moment transforms into light.

The Concealed Comforts

In the corner, a cat takes a nap,
While I'm battling a snack attack.
Socks tossed high on a chair with flair,
Life's oddities dance in my cozy lair.

A spoonful of chaos in a bowl of bliss,
My chaotic home, I would never miss.
Fluffy cushions act as my trusty throne,
With jokes on the walls that make me groan.

Dust bunnies tumble like jesters bold,
Tales of my sandwich habit never get old.
In this fortress, we laugh, we thrive,
Together in madness, oh what a vibe!

So let the world swirl, let it spin,
In this cozy retreat, I'm ready to win.
With laughter and snacks, it's a whimsical spree,
My secret haven, just my cat and me.

Safe Within the Confines

Walls painted bright, like a circus show,
Where toys come alive when nobody's low.
A fridge that hums a mischievous tune,
Guess what? Leftovers dance under the moon!

Pajamas my armor, I wear them with pride,
In a fortress of snacks, I call my inside.
A fortress of blankets, my fort is a maze,
Lost in the cushions, in a delicious daze.

Awkward selfies adorn my walls,
With funny faces that never appall.
My coffee cups hold stories untold,
In this quirky nook, I'm never too bold.

So here I shall stay, with a grin ear to ear,
Binge-watching shows, avoiding all fear.
In the heart of my chaos, a sketchy delight,
Safe where the silliness shines oh so bright.

Embrace of Structured Solitude

Within these confines, I dance with glee,
An opera of socks and my cup of tea.
Books stacked high, like towers of fun,
In the land of quiet, I can be the pun.

Waffles on Sunday, my culinary feat,
Dancing with syrup, oh, what a treat!
Jokes in the margins of my favorite reads,
In this structured solitude, I'm planting my seeds.

Spaghetti on Mondays, a noodle-like art,
As I twirl my fork, it transforms into a dart.
With laughter as fuel, I fuel my day,
In this charming haven, I'm happy to stay.

Mirrors reflect my most silly sides,
With hairdos that sway like a wild, fun ride.
Here, I'm a monarch of humorous bliss,
In a castle of giggles, I'll reminisce.

Bound by Brick and Mortar

Bricks and laughter make a sturdy frame,
In this cozy chaos, I've staked my claim.
Dancing with shadows, I twirl like a fool,
In the playground of comfort, I've made my rule.

Walls that echo with chuckles and cheer,
Whispers of secrets, no need to adhere.
A bailarina spins in a sea of socks,
While popcorn kernels plot tricks in their box.

Here, the mailman delivers pure jest,
With packages of giggles, a quirky fest.
Chasing the dust motes that waltz in the air,
In this brick-bound haven, I've found my flair.

So let the world whirl, let it swirl around,
In my fortress of fabrics, new joys will abound.
Each crack in the walls holds a joke or two,
In this brick and mortar, I'm always brand new.

Underneath the Roof's Protection

In a cozy nook where the cat does snore,
I kick my shoes off, and who needs more?
The couch is my throne, the snack bowl's near,
This fortress of blankets, it brings me cheer.

The ceiling may leak, the walls may creak,
But this place of refuge is all that I seek.
With pizza on lap and remote in hand,
In my little kingdom, I'm in command.

The Sanctuary of Stillness

Inside these four walls, I plot and I scheme,
Creating wild worlds, living the dream.
With a cup of warm tea and a blanket to share,
I giggle at thoughts that dance in the air.

The fridge calls my name with a knowing grin,
The snacks are my pals, they let the fun begin.
No one to judge as I belt out a tune,
In my sanctuary, I'm a pop-star croon.

Nestled in Quiet Corners

In my corner of chaos, I giggle and grin,
With mismatched socks, let the fun begin!
Books piled like mountains, adventures await,
I dive into stories, it's never too late.

With dust bunnies soft, they dance in the light,
They bob and they weave—such a comical sight!
Here in my haven, all worries take flight,
Joy's just a tickle, and laughter's the right.

Whispers of the Enclosed

Behind these stout walls, the laughter flows free,
Where shenanigans dance like a raucous spree.
The dog wears a hat, the goldfish joins in,
With antics so goofy, it's a whirlwind spin.

Cushions become castles, the floor is a sea,
And I'm the brave captain, come mess with me!
With each silly moment, I laugh till I drop,
In this whimsical space, I never want to stop.

The Protective Veil of Privacy

In a world of chatter, I sit real still,
Where whispers of neighbors invade my chill.
I wear my pajamas, a mask of delight,
Perfectly hidden from day into night.

The cat's my accomplice, we plan our escape,
From a land full of noise, we fashion our tape.
With snacks piled high and the TV on blast,
Who needs the outside? We're having a blast!

The mailman delivers, but I just pretend,
That my fortress of boxes will never quite end.
With curtains drawn tight, I clinch my first prize,
In this wacky world, I wear my disguise.

So here I will stay, in my cozy retreat,
Where chaos is handled from my cushy seat.
The allure of the world is far, far away,
In my bubble of privacy, I'm here to stay.

Garden of Intimate Silence

In my backyard kingdom, the flowers all talk,
With petals that giggle, they circle the clock.
The weeds spread rumors, they whisper with glee,
While I sip my lemonade, just wild and free.

The fence is my curtain, the birds are my choir,
Each note a reminder, I'm here to retire.
The grass grows in patches, a plush velvet sea,
Where gossip and laughter can blossom with glee.

The tomatoes are blushing, they're all in a race,
To share juicy secrets in this sacred place.
Garden gnomes nod slowly; they're wise and discreet,
In my intimate silence, life feels quite sweet.

So let the winds carry the tales from the trees,
Where giggles abound and time moves with ease.
In this quirky domain, I'll dance all day long,
In my garden of silence, where I truly belong.

Retreating into the Known

When I close my door, the world's on mute,
With snacks in the pantry, I take a reclute.
Netflix and blankets, a perfect alliance,
Who needs real life when there's couch-reliance?

My phone may ring loud, but I click it off,
Let them leave messages, I'll never scoff.
I hide in plain sight, like a ninja at play,
In the fortress of comfort, I frolic all day.

The fridge is a treasure, its bounty immense,
With leftovers laughing and making their scents.
I become a chef in this solo delight,
Inventing strange dishes that might cause a fright.

So here I will linger, in my happy cocoon,
Where mundane annoyances are silenced too soon.
In the realm of the known, I'm the king, what a thrill,
With retreat as my mantra, I'm feasting at will!

Enveloped by the Boundaries

A boundary of pillows, snug as a bug,
In my fortress of fluff, I give the world a shrug.
The outside is wild, but here it's all neat,
With cereal castles and socks on my feet.

Neighbors just wonder what shenanigans brew,
As I plot my escape to the land of the zoo.
The dog rolls his eyes while I dance with my tea,
In this castle of chaos, it's just him and me.

The walls hold my laughter, the ceilings my sighs,
As I create mischief beneath all the skies.
World View on pause while I broaden my grin,
In my whimsical haven, the fun's about to begin.

Here in my bubble, a true comedy show,
With dreams that take flight and worries that flow.
Wrapped in these boundaries, I giggle and play,
In the land of my making, I'll happily stay!

www.ingramcontent.com/pod-product-compliance
Lightning Source LLC
Chambersburg PA
CBHW051732290426
43661CB00122B/236